RAPID

Assessment Handbook: The Rapid Route to Raising Attainment

Welcome to your **Raising Attainment Guide** for **Rapid**, the programme designed to help struggling learners aged 7-11 make rapid progress in **Reading**, **Writing** and **Maths**.

Using your Assesment Handbook

The value of assessment

When you are working with children who are having difficulties, good assessment is invaluable. Good assessment helps children see that they are making progress and helps you to identify where they need further support and practice, as well as enabling you to praise them for what they've achieved. It is also a great medium for reassuring parents and carers about their child's progress and creating a positive attitude about the child's learning for all who are involved in it.

Children's self-assessment

Children learn best when they are encouraged to reflect on their own learning. Rapid supports children in self-assessment in a variety of ways:

- Rapid Maths: use the Record Sheets at the end of each colour level's Teaching Guide
- Rapid Writing: ask children to colour in the self-assessment 'thumbs' on each Writing Log page
- Rapid Reading: encourage children to complete the My Reading Progress charts on pages 8 or 11 of this Handbook

The Rapid software for each subject has a certificate that you can print off for children; you can also use the certificate of achievement at the end of this Handbook to reward children and keep motivation high.

How to use this Handbook

This guide is designed to help you place children at the correct level within Rapid Reading, Rapid Writing and Rapid Maths. It will enable you to keep a regular track of how they are progressing, and be able to demonstrate the progress they are making. You can use the charts and trackers here to share this evidence with other adults involved in the child's learning. There are also opportunities to share this information with the children themselves and celebrate their successes.

Choose Reading, Writing or Maths and turn to the appropriate section of the Handbook

↓

Record the child's current level of achievement according to your professional judgement, and other teachers' assessments if appropriate, to set a baseline

↓

Use the Rapid assessment for that subject to confirm at which point in the programme the child can confidently work

↓

Group together children of a similar ability using a combination of your own knowledge of their strengths and weaknesses and group dynamics, the Rapid assessments, and National Curriculum levelling

↓

Start using the Rapid books and software regularly (at least twice a week is recommended)

↓

Use the Progress Tracker charts in this Handbook to keep a track of children's progress at the regular intervals recommended for each subject: i.e. for Rapid Reading, at the end of each Set; for Rapid Maths at the end of each Part of a colour level and for Rapid Writing at the end of each Writing Log. For Rapid Writing, there is also an unaided writing assessment that you can use termly or half-termly

Rapid Reading

Rapid Reading consists of finely graded reading books, each containing two texts (one fiction, one non-fiction). It is divided into **two Starter levels** and **six main Stages**. Each Stage is further divided into Set A or Set B. This fine levelling gives children the small but important steps they need in order to progress with confidence and security in their reading skills. In order to secure excellent progress, children must read the books with an adult and then practise their reading using the software.

Rapid Reading Level	Book band	Reading Age	England and Wales National Curriculum Level	Scottish CfE Level	Northern Ireland Curriculum Level	Catch Up Level
Starter 1 Set A or B	Red	5.0–5.3	P7/8	Early	Within Level 1	2
Starter 2 Set A or B	Yellow	5.4–5.5	P8	Early	Within Level 1	3
Stage 1 Set A or B	Blue	5.6–5.11	1c	First	Towards Level 2	4
Stage 2 Set A or B	Green	6.0–6.5	1b	First	Towards Level 2	5
Stage 3 Set A or B	Orange	6.6–6.11	1a	First	Within Level 2	6
Stage 4 Set A or B	Turquoise	7.0–7.5	2c	First	Within Level 2	7
Stage 5 Set A or B	Purple	7.6–7.11	2b	First	Within Level 2	8
Stage 6 Set A or B	Gold	8.0–8.5	2a/3c	First	Within Level 2	9

Placing children in the Rapid Reading programme

When you have a new child starting on the Rapid Reading programme, whether they are new to the programme or new to your class, follow the steps below to ensure that they are on the right path to achieving and feeling more confident in reading.

Child is identified as needing extra support.

↓

Record child's National Curriculum reading level (using class teacher's assessment) or Scottish/Northen Ireland equivalent.

↓

Record child's reading age using a standardised reading test.

↓

Ask the child to read the Benchmark Book for the appropriate Stage and Set and carry out the Running Record found in the Teacher Guide.

↓

A child at Rapid Stage 1–3 with five miscues or fewer can progress to the next stage. A child at Rapid Stage 4–6 with 10 miscues or fewer can progress to the next Stage/Set.

↓

If more than 10 miscues, child should read within that Stage/Set.

↓

Repeat Benchmark Book assessment each time child finishes a Set.

↓

Record NC level and reading age termly.

Use the 'My Reading Progress' charts on pages 8 or 11 and the Key Word Assessment lists on pages 9, 10, 12 or 13 to check children's ability to read key words and help them feel in control of their own learning.

Diagnostic assessment using Rapid Reading Running records

Rapid Reading has an integral Assessment strand which is both formative and summative. It can be used to:

- place a child within the programme
- check whether the child is ready to move up to the next Set of the programme
- provide ongoing tracking of the child's reading performance.

The Assessment strand has two elements:

1. The **Benchmark Books** and corresponding **Running Record** proformas
2. **Comprehension**, **Phonics** and **Spelling** proformas

All the proformas can be found in the *Rapid Reading* Teaching Guides pages 98–109.

Assessing a child using the Benchmark Book and the Comprehension, Phonics and Spelling assessment

1. Select the **Benchmark Book** for the appropriate Stage and Set. Each Benchmark Book contains two stories. The first story is used to assess performance when a child has read all the texts of Set A, and the second story is used when a child has read all the texts of Set B. The stories feature the same characters children have met in the other stories in the Set so there is continuity between teaching, learning and assessment.
2. Photocopy the relevant **Running Record proforma** and **Comprehension**, **Phonics** and **Spelling proforma** from the Teaching Guide.
3. Introduce the story to the child in the usual way, using the Before Reading page.
4. Ask the child to read aloud to you. As they are reading, use the **Running Record proforma** to score all words read correctly; all omissions; all insertions and all errors.
5. When the child has read the story, check comprehension, phonic knowledge and spelling by using the Quiz page. The questions on the Quiz page are reproduced on the **Comprehension**, **Phonics** and **Spelling proforma**. Give the child a score according to the scoring guidance.
6. Later, tally the number of errors noted on the **Running Record proforma** and use the table on page 95 of the Teaching Guide to identify the accuracy rate. Then tally the score the child achieved on the **Comprehension**, **Phonics** and **Spelling assessment**.

   The results of these two assessments will determine whether the child is ready to move to the next level of *Rapid Reading*.
7. By reviewing the completed Running Record it will be possible to see if a child is consistently making similar errors, e.g.

   a) unable to blend phonemes to read words (phonic weakness)
   b) says words that do no make sense in the sentence (comprehension weakness)

   Identifying patterns of errors will help target areas for further practice (using *Rapid Reading* software).

RAPID

Example of a completed *Rapid* Running Record

RW means Running Words. This is the number of words being assessed.

Name: Michael Date: 12 October

Story: **Rugby Run** RW = 50

Page	*Shaded words are not assessed*	Strategies used	Words assessed • = miscues
7	“I can stop him,” said Tom. (stop: s-o-t; said: T) “No, Tom,” said Kim. “The man is too big. (too: OSc) You can’t stop him.” (can’t: can)	Ph G	I can stop • him said • no the man is too big you can’t •
8	Tom ran at the robber. (ran: r-a-n Ph Sc) The robber ran fast, but Tom ran faster.	Ph	ran at but
9	Tom got the robber. “Got you!” he said. “Aaargh!” said the robber.		got he
10	A policeman saw Tom. (saw: was) “Good job, Tom,” (Good: G; job: T) said the policeman. “I saw you stop the robber.”	G G	a saw • good • job
11	“Good job, Tom,” said Kim. (Good: Go...Sc) “You got the robber. You can run fast.”		
12	“Yes,” said Tom. “I can run fast.” “I *am* good at rugby!”		

Key:
T = told O = omitted Sc = self-corrects
Strategies: Ph = phonic G = graphic S = syntactic C = contextual

Total miscues: 5

Example of a completed *Rapid* Comprehension, Phonics and Spelling Record

Name: Michael Date: 12 October

Story: Rugby Run

Text Detective

Questions to check understanding **Response (1 – 3)**

Literal recall
What did the robber steal from the lady?
He stole her handbag. [3]

Inferential comprehension
Why did Tom say he was good at rugby?
Because he could run fast and he was good at tackling. [3]

Personal response
Do you think Tom was brave?
Yes, because he tackled the man (does not say the man was big). [2]

Response Key: 3 = Excellent 2 = Average 1 = Weak

Word Detective

Phonics (0 – 1)

Phonic Assessment: Blending three phonemes

Page 8: Sound out the three phonemes (sounds) in 'ran'. Can you blend them? [0]

Page 9: Sound out the three phonemes (sounds) in 'got'. Can you blend them? [1]

Page 10: Sound out the three phonemes (sounds) in 'job'. Can you blend them? [1]

Response Key: 0 = No 1 = Yes

Super Speller

Spelling (0 – 1)

Can you spell these words from memory?

Word	Pupil's spelling	Score
you	you	0
stop	stop	1
saw	saw	1

Response Key: 0 = No 1 = Yes

Reading Level

Accuracy rate = 90 % Comprehension, Phonics and Spelling score = 12 /15

What Next?

5 miscues or fewer and 7+ for comprehension – move to next *Rapid* level.
If pupil scores below this – continue at this *Rapid* level and consider the following:

Michael is ready for Stage 2 Set B.

Problem	**Solution**
Some sight words not recognised	Use Writing PCMs for further practice
Hesitant and robotic reading	Demonstrate reading with pace and intonation
	Use 'Read and Record' feature on *Rapid Reading Assistant* Software
Comprehension weak	Paired reading of texts and encourage discussion
	Listen to 'Read to Me' feature on *Rapid Reading Assistant* Software
Phonic knowledge uncertain	Use Phonics PCMs for further practice
Spelling inaccurate	Further practice with 'Look Say Cover Write Check'

Name: ____________________ Date: ____________________

My Reading Progress Chart

Series 1/2 Stage 1 Set A

Key words
- ☐ I can read all 10 words on List 1A.

Phonics
- ☐ I can hear a phoneme at the beginning of a word.
- ☐ I can write the phoneme at the beginning of a word.

Comprehension
- ☐ I can remember what I have read.
- ☐ I can talk about what I have read.

Reading style
- ☐ I can pause when I see a full stop.

Series 1/2 Stage 1 Set B

Key words
- ☐ I can read all 10 words on List 1B.

Phonics
- ☐ I can hear a phoneme at the end of a word.
- ☐ I know two letters can make one sound.

Comprehension
- ☐ I can remember what I have read.
- ☐ I can talk about what I have read.

Reading style
- ☐ I can pause when I see a full stop.

Series 1/2 Stage 2 Set A

Key words
- ☐ I can read all 15 words on List 2A.

Phonics
- ☐ I can blend three-phoneme words.
- ☐ I can write some three-letter words.

Comprehension
- ☐ I can remember what I have read.
- ☐ I can answer questions about what I have read.

Reading style
- ☐ I always pause when I see a full stop.

Series 1/2 Stage 2 Set B

Key words
- ☐ I can read all 15 words on List 2B.

Phonics
- ☐ I can hear the phoneme in the middle of a three-letter word.
- ☐ I can write most three-letter words.

Comprehension
- ☐ I can remember what I have read.
- ☐ I can answer questions about what I have read.

Reading style
- ☐ I always pause when I see a full stop.

Series 1/2 Stage 3 Set A

Key words
- ☐ I can read all 20 words on List 3A.

Phonics
- ☐ I can blend two consonants at the beginning of a word.
- ☐ I can write some words which start with two consonants.

Comprehension
- ☐ I can guess what will happen at the end of a story.
- ☐ I can remember new facts from my reading.

Reading style
- ☐ I can change my voice for different characters.

Series 1/2 Stage 3 Set B

Key words
- ☐ I can read all 20 words on List 3B.

Phonics
- ☐ I can blend two consonants at the end of a word.
- ☐ I can write some words which end with two consonants.

Comprehension
- ☐ I can guess what will happen at the end of a story.
- ☐ I can remember new facts from my reading.

Reading style
- ☐ I can change my voice for questions and exclamation marks.

Key Word assessment: Series 1 Stages 1–3

List 1A	List 1B	List 2A	List 2B	List 3A	List 3B
at	he	big	are	were	could
in	go	see	very	put	full
is	to	has	down	one	more
it	the	saw	must	looked	from
on	got	his	our	for	made
and	but	said	some	away	your
had	can	with	want	off	their
did	will	him	went	wanted	eat
yes	was	like	came	lots	again
me	not	here	they	does	so
		you	this	most	where
		stop	get	think	took
		out	that	gave	what
		have	old	then	live
		all	into	fast	home
				coming	who
				jumped	her
				would	there
				now	just
				open	half

List 1A

by
we
us
if
sat
cat
up
job
help
look

List 1B

cut
do
fed
of
ran
yet
bit
no
dog
fun

List 2A

thing
mad
man
play
be
swim
am
bad
star
far
stay
shop
make
boy
fell

List 2B

take
wet
pick
goes
find
how
try
way
she
run
didn't
let
show
pull
walked

List 3A

cold
send
space
turned
wait
day
work
head
school
still
sorry
hard
became
lost
round
comes
began
ever
tiny
tall

List 3B

best
kept
played
become
when
running
can't
shut
keep
give
need
isn't
four
real
those
asked
buy
opened
bite
sitting

Name: ____________________ Date: ____________________

My Reading Progress Chart

Series 1/2 Stage 4 Set A

Key words
- ☐ I can read all 20 words on List 4A.

Phonics
- ☐ I can hear a long vowel phoneme in the middle of a word.
- ☐ I can say the long vowel phoneme in the middle of a word.

Comprehension
- ☐ I can predict what will happen next in a story.
- ☐ I can ask and answer simple questions.

Reading style
- ☐ I can read with expression.

Series 1/2 Stage 4 Set B

Key words
- ☐ I can read all 20 words on List 4B.

Phonics
- ☐ I can hear a long vowel phoneme in the middle of a word.
- ☐ I can write some words with long vowel phonemes.

Comprehension
- ☐ I can predict what will happen next in a story.
- ☐ I can ask and answer simple questions.

Reading style
- ☐ I use punctuation to help my reading.

Series 1/2 Stage 5 Set A

Key words
- ☐ I can read all 20 words on List 5A.

Phonics
- ☐ I know to drop the 'e' before adding 'ing' to some verbs.
- ☐ I can write some verbs with 'ing'.

Comprehension
- ☐ I can retell a story in sequence.
- ☐ I can pick out important facts on a page.

Reading style
- ☐ I can read aloud quite quickly and accurately.

Series 1/2 Stage 5 Set B

Key words
- ☐ I can read all 20 words on List 5B.

Phonics
- ☐ I know to double a consonant before adding 'ing' to some verbs.
- ☐ I can write some verbs with a double consonant and 'ing'.

Comprehension
- ☐ I can retell a story in sequence.
- ☐ I can pick out important facts on a page.

Reading style
- ☐ I know how to read a word if it is in bold or italics.

Series 1/2 Stage 6 Set A

Key words
- ☐ I can read all 20 words on List 6A.

Phonics
- ☐ I can blend two consonants at the beginning of a word.
- ☐ I can write some words which start with two consonants.

Comprehension
- ☐ I can find evidence to support my thinking.
- ☐ I can find the main points of a non-fiction text.

Reading style
- ☐ I can read aloud fiction fluently.

Series 1/2 Stage 6 Set B

Key words
- ☐ I can read all 20 words on List 6B.

Phonics
- ☐ I can hear an unstressed vowel in a two-syllable word.
- ☐ I can remember to write letters in a word even if I can't hear them.

Comprehension
- ☐ I can find evidence to support my thinking.
- ☐ I can find the main points of a non-fiction text.

Reading style
- ☐ I can read aloud non-fiction fluently.

Key Word assessment: Series 1 Stages 4–6

List 4A

back
don't
going
small
them
catch
around
pushed
used
inside
time
next
lived
three
worked
high
every
across
late
slow

List 4B

little
when
right
many
start
along
ate
trying
years
gone
cannot
always
knew
asked
move
house
cross
strong
great
each

List 5A

after
over
two
called
about
good
putting
shopping
sorry
later
choose
please
write
before
having
today
other
forgot
using
everything

List 5B

any
wasn't
under
light
soon
really
never
something
cried
things
quick
angry
stopped
getting
carry
near
first
making
should
both

List 6A

anything
morning
thought
someone
appear
seeing
sure
friend
until
another
tried
sometimes
know
doing
nothing
these
also
last
found
people

List 6B

believe
only
watch
family
terrible
enough
quite
shout
because
standing
climbed
might
together
surprise
talk
alone
suddenly
perhaps
bought
through

Key Word assessment: Series 2 Stages 4–6

List 4A

throw
sleep
fight
loud
night
often
landed
shouted
bigger
fly
being
wear
food
quiet
cook
idea
dinner
class
loved
dropped

List 4B

missing
much
own
talking
couldn't
done
follow
school
swing
change
strange
outside
place
crept
saving
water
even
taking
carried
fallen

List 5A

slowly
clever
scared
lose
huge
hear
lifted
yelled
clean
myself
anyway
tired
sold
himself
lucky
name
ready
drink
hoping
stepped

List 5B

wrote
died
trapped
bring
check
spoke
wrong
secret
same
touch
noise
meant
anyone
hiding
leave
drive
careful
washing
bright
which

List 6A

nobody
somebody
flew
afraid
everyone
nowhere
above
listen
pulled
speak
wild
front
eyes
behind
raced
different
almost
below
anywhere
large

List 6B

yourself
easy
already
doesn't
caught
laughed
anybody
tomorrow
problem
closed
living
remember
weather
hungry
ground
heard
dreamed
favourite
finished
half

Pupil name ____________ Term ____ TA name ____________

Pupil Progress Tracker

Date	Rapid Stage and Set	Book title Text title	Notes about reading	PCM completed?	Software session completed?

Group name ____________________ **Term** ______ **TA name** __________________

Group Progress Tracker

Child's name	NC level at start	Target NC level	Rapid Reading Stage and Set at start	Rapid Reading Stage and Set at end	Stage and Set difference	Reading age (y:m) at start	Reading age (y:m) at end	Reading age difference	Number of sessions

Yearly Progress Tracker

Name:________________________	Rapid Stage and Set	NC sub-level	Reading age (y:m)
Term 1			
Term 2			
Term 3			
Term 4			
Term 5			
Term 6			
Name:________________________	Rapid Stage and Set	NC sub-level	Reading age (y:m)
Term 1			
Term 2			
Term 3			
Term 4			
Term 5			
Term 6			
Name:________________________	Rapid Stage and Set	NC sub-level	Reading age (y:m)
Term 1			
Term 2			
Term 3			
Term 4			
Term 5			
Term 6			
Name:________________________	Rapid Stage and Set	NC sub-level	Reading age (y:m)
Term 1			
Term 2			
Term 3			
Term 4			
Term 5			
Term 6			

Note: This chart is based on a six-term year (six half terms).

Rapid Writing

Rapid Writing is a programme of guided writing sessions covering all writing skills:

- spelling
- punctuation
- grammar
- sentence structure
- writing for purpose and audience.

Rapid Writing is divided into **three Stages** and **nine Writing Logs**. The Writing Logs alternate fiction and non-fiction, and there is a gradual increase in difficulty. The materials are designed to build children's writing skills in short bursts, so that they can apply these skills to longer pieces of writing back in the classroom. In order to secure excellent progress, children should take part in the guided writing session and then practise their writing skills using the software.

Rapid Writing Stage	Rapid Writing Log	England and Wales National Curriculum Level	Scottish CfE Level	Northern Ireland Curriculum Level
Stage 1	Writing Log 1	P8–1c	Early	Within Level 1
	Writing Log 2	1c–1b	First	Towards Level 2
	Writing Log 3	1a	First	Within Level 2
Stage 2	Writing Log 4	1a–2c	First	Within Level 2
	Writing Log 5	2c	First	Within Level 2
	Writing Log 6	2b	First	Within Level 2
Stage 3	Writing Log 7	2b	First	Within Level 2
	Writing Log 8	2b–2a	First	Within Level 2
	Writing Log 9	2a–3c	First	Within Level 2

Placing children in the Rapid Writing programme

When you have a new child starting on the Rapid Writing programme, whether they are new to the programme or new to your class, follow the steps below to ensure that they are on the right path to achieving and feeling more confident in writing.

Child is identified as needing extra support.

↓

Record the child's National Curriculum writing level (using class teacher's assessment) or Scottish/Northern Ireland equivalent.

↓

Ask the child to carry out an unaided Placement Assessment (page 19 of this guide).

↓

Mark it using the mark scheme on pages 20–21.

↓

Follow the recommendations given in the mark scheme.

↓

Review progress using the materials in the Rapid Writing programme: Independent Writing assessments (after 5 units) and Guided Writing assessments (after 10 units).

↓

Carry out an unaided Placement Assessment after 10 units, choosing a different prompt each time.

↓

Record NC level for writing after 10 units.

Note: In a six-term year, 5 units is equal to a term.

Rapid Writing Placement Assessments

These Placement Assessments can be used whatever level the children are working at. You can use them to work out which Writing Log the child should start at; you could then use them every 10 units to build up a picture of their progress. They will reveal the areas of strength and weakness, which will add to your professional judgement of their writing ability.

Carrying out the Placement Assessments

- Allow each child **20 minutes** for the task.
- Give each child a fresh sheet of paper.
- Read the writing prompts choices to the children: **My Best Day**; **The Naughty Puppy**; **The Mysterious Box**. Ask them to choose which one they would like to write about.
- When the children have chosen, write the title for them at the top of their paper. Then say something like: *I wonder what exciting story you could write about that? I'm going to see how well you can do all on your own, so have a go and do your best!*
- If a child specifically asks for help, be encouraging but don't help! Say: *It doesn't matter if you don't get all the spellings right, just try to write the word and that will be fine.*
- If children at the lower ability levels become tired before 20 minutes, prompt them gently to continue, but do not feel they have to continue for the full 20 minutes.

Using the mark scheme

The mark scheme on pages 20–21 is designed to be used with the Placement Assessments listed above, but it can also be used for any piece of unaided writing. Use your knowledge of each child's National Curriculum level to choose which sheet to start with. If you are unsure, or if a child is on the borderline between 1a and 2c, use both sheets together. Work through the sheet in order, scoring 1 point for each feature demonstrated in the child's writing. Total all the scores, and refer to the box on the right-hand side of Sheet 2 to see which Writing Log the child should start at.

Don't forget:

- A child might have characteristics of a sub-level or two above or below the estimated NC level of the piece.
- Any one sample of writing will only reveal some of the listed skills. A full picture of the child's ability will emerge over a range of writing tasks.
- The recommended Writing Log may start at a slightly lower level than the child's writing ability. This will form useful revision and consolidation of skills and can serve to bolster children's confidence. If, after a few sessions, the child is clearly capable of writing at a higher level, consider moving them up a group.

Writing mark scheme: Sheet 1

NC	Overall meaning	
P8	Can say what they intend to write	
P8	Can recall what they have written	
1c	Content has some logic	
1c	Can read back some of their writing	
1b	Message is generally clear	
1b	Can read back most of their writing	
1a	Message is clear	
1a	Ideas are linked	
	total	

NC	Use of genre	
P8	Can write caption for a picture / Can write a single idea news piece	
1c	Recounts answer who and what / Stories link two ideas	
1b	Recounts connect three events e.g. who, what and where / Stories have character(s) and some limited action	
1b	Some features of genre	
1a	Genre is generally sustained throughout piece	
1a	Recounts may answer who, what, when and where / Stories have character(s) and several actions	
	total	

NC	Grammar	
P8	Pupils write words	
1c	Some 'sentences' do not have missing words	
1c	Writing is in 'sentences' (although not all demarcated)	
1b	Most 'sentences' do not have missing words	
1b	Most writing is in simple 'sentences'	
1a	Simple sentences have subject/verb agreement	
1a	Some compound sentences	
	total	

NC	Punctuation	
1c	Some sentences start with a capital letter	
1b	Some sentences have a capital letter and a full stop	
1a	Simple sentences have a capital letter and a full stop and possibly question mark	
1a	Question marks are usually used	
	total	

NC	Vocabulary	
1c	Echoes spoken language	
1c	Uses mainly key words	
1b	Echoes spoken language but evidence of langauge of genre (little, old / First you)	
1b	Uses mainly key words but some evidence of adjectives	
1a	Some formulaic phrases e.g. Once upon a time, One day	
1a	Some evidence of word selection	
	total	

NC	Spelling	
P8	Can spell some words e.g. a, I, it	
1c	Spells approx. 15 high frequency words correctly e.g. the, he	
1c	Spells most cvc words correctly e.g. but, man	
1b	Spells approx. 25 high frequency words correctly e.g. you, was	
1b	Spells simple monosyllabic words correctly e.g. will, help	
1a	Spells approx. 35 irregular high frequency words correctly e.g. they, have	
1a	Spells most phonically regular monosyllabic words correctly e.g. shop, feet	
	total	

NC	Handwriting	
P8	Forms a few letters correctly	
P8	Can write own name	
1c	Usually leaves spaces between words	
1c	Forms some letters correctly	
1b	Forms many letters correctly	
1b	Most letters correctly orientated to line	
1a	Forms most letters correctly	
1a	Letters are generally even in size	
	total	

NC	Length of writing	
P8	Approx. 20 words	
1c	Approx. 40 words	
1b	Approx. 60 words	
1a	Approx. 80 words	
	total	

Writing mark scheme: Sheet 2

NC	Overall meaning	
2c	Sequence is logical	
2c	Some ideas are developed	
2b	Ideas are sequenced and developed	
2b	Some details are added	
2a	Writing relates to title	
2a	Mostly holds the reader's attention	
3c	Ideas are grouped	
3c	Holds the reader's attention	
	total	

NC	Use of genre	
2c	Recounts told in time order with First, Next etc. / Stories have formulaic beginning, middle and end	
2b	Mostly accurate genre features for recounts and instructions / Stories have deliberate beginning, middle and end	
2a	Accurate genre features for stories, recounts and instructions	
3c	Writing shows some originality	
	total	

NC	Grammar	
2c	Simple and compound sentences show consistency in tense	
2c	Dialogue is introduced in fiction/ cause and effect statements in non-fiction	
2b	Some complex sentences	
2b	Some variation in sentence openings	
2a	More evidence of complex sentences	
2a	Wider variation in sentence openings	
3c	Complex sentences with a range of cohesive devices	
3c	Variety of sentence structure	
	total	

NC	Punctuation	
2c	Simple sentences mostly correctly punctuated	
2c	Some compound sentences correctly punctuated	
2b	Most simple and compound sentences correctly punctuated, possibly including exclamation marks	
2a	Most simple, compound and complex sentences accurately punctuated	
3c	Beginning and end sentence punctuation accurate	
3c	Some use of speech marks / Commas in lists	
	total	

NC	Vocabulary	
2c	Some use of adjectives	
2c	Some formulaic descriptions, e.g. yummy dinner	
2b	A few words chosen for effect e.g. strong verbs	
2b	Increase of 'story' type words e.g. little, old man	
2a	Some adventurous word choices / more technical vocabulary in non-fiction	
2a	Less use of 'writing as they speak'	
3c	More adventurous word choices	
3c	More evidence of writing to engage reader	
	total	

NC	Spelling	
2c	Spells approx. 50 irregular high frequency words correctly e.g. what, want	
2c	Spells phonically regular monosyllabic words correctly e.g. rain, make	
2b	Spells approx. 75 irregular high frequency words correctly e.g. come, does	
2b	Spells many phonically regular words correctly e.g. across	
2a	Spells approx. 100 irregular high frequency words correctly e.g. once, other	
2a	Spells most phonically regular correctly e.g. right	
3c	Spells approx. 125 irregular high frequency words correctly e.g. their, coming	
3c	Spells phonically words regular correctly e.g. cried	
	total	

NC	Handwriting	
2c	Forms all letters correctly and most letters are even in size and correctly orientated	
2b	Letters, including capitals, are correctly formed and orientated	
2a	Mostly legible and neat	
3c	Writing is mostly legible, neat and looks fluent	
	total	

NC	Length of writing	
2c	More than 100 words	
2b	More than 125 words	
2a	More than 150 words	
3c	More than 200 words	
	total	

Total from sheet 1	
Total from sheet 2	
Overall total	

Score	Writing Log to start on	Indicative NC level
0 to 4	Not suitable for Rapid Writing	below P8
5 to 8	Writing Log 1	P8
9 to 21	Writing Log 1	1c
21 to 35	Writing Log 2	1b
36 to 42	Writing Log 3	1a
43 to 50	Writing Log 4	1a
51 to 63	Writing Log 5	2c
64 to 69	Writing Log 6	2b
70 to 75	Writing Log 7	2b
75 to 87	Writing Log 8	2a
88 to 100	Writing Log 9	3c

Writing samples

Scarlet, Writing Log 1, NC level 1c

My ~~bestday~~ ~~best day~~ My best day is going to the fer because ther's roler costurs and splashy writer rids but sume time's it is verry ~~chit~~ cheerfull and am verry contented but went on the ~~rolco~~ roler costur my Fat Face turnt red and I screemd my head OFF and ther was a ginormous wile I went on it and it went wrond and wrownd I got stuck and my mum and dad pulled and puled I hade got ~~out~~ ~~out~~ out and we went on a writur ried I Shouted can I get OFF NOW it hade a nufe I code not get OFF until it was Finishd it took hurf a awer and then it was time to go Home we Hade hot choclet on the way home× I hade a little sleep in the ~~mi~~ miny bus× the End.

Overall meaning
The overall meaning of Scarlet's recount, describing a trip to the fair, has some logic but the message is not always clear. (1c = 3)

Use of genre
The recount answers 'what' ('who' and 'where' are mentioned in general terms).
It starts in the present tense but then does settle into consistent use of the past tense. (1c = 2)

Grammar
Scarlet's writing is in 'sentences' but sometimes words are missing. (1c = 2)

Punctuation
Scarlet's writing is more like a spoken account and she has not used sentence punctuation. (0)

Vocabulary
She shows some use of adjectives and descriptive language, e.g. 'ginormous', 'my face went red'. (1b = 4)

Spelling
Scarlet is able to spell some high-frequency words 'went', 'was' and some phonically regular monosyllabic words 'stuck', 'took'. However, she is still making errors on other high-frequency words, e.g. 'ther' 'hade'. (1c = 3)

Handwriting
Scarlet forms some letters correctly, though her writing is sometimes difficult to read and her letters are not uniform in size and capitals are used inappropriately. (1c = 4)

Length of writing
Scarlett has managed to write more than 100 words. (2c = 5)

Total score: 23
Overall, although Scarlett is approximately working at NC level 1c, her lack of sentence punctuation means she would benefit from working on Writing Log 1.

Writing samples

Ben, Writing Log 2, NC level 1b

The Mysterious Box

One day I found a box in the back garden. The box was unushrul. I opend the box there was nuthing in it. Ecsept for a stone a unushul stone in a unushrul box. Just then the stone came to Life I blinck and the box came to Life. a While later I fugot the Stone and the box then we were frends.

Overall meaning
Ben's story has some logic but the ideas are undeveloped. (1c = 3)

Use of genre
He is attempting a mystery story but there is very limited action and the ending strays away from the genre. (1c = 2)

Grammar
Ben has some control over writing in sentences which have subject/verb agreement. (1a = 6)

Punctuation
50% of Ben's sentences are accurately punctuated. (1b = 2)

Vocabulary
He uses some formulaic phrases 'One day' and there is some evidence of word selection: 'Except for a stone' 'just then'. (1a = 4)

Spelling
Ben's spelling shows some accuracy: 'found' 'garden' 'later' and he makes good phonic attempts at less familiar words 'unushrul' 'fugot'. (1a = 6)

Handwriting
While his letters are mostly well formed he is not consistent with use of upper- and lower-case letters. (1c = 3)

Length of writing
Ben was only able to write approximately 60 words in the 20 minutes allowed. (1b = 3)

Total score: 29
Overall, Ben is working within NC level 1b and should work on Writing Log 2.

Ethan, Writing Log 3, NC level 1a

My Best Day

my Best day was when i did my Best run in cross cutrey and i cam 42 and my dad and mum wur verey happey. So thay let me Biy some swets and thay wur choits thay wur yumey and I ate them ~~t t~~ all. ~~up~~ then I hat to go home so i did and plad on the PS3 and pade Kesar 11 it was fun then i ate my timur was yumey. and i ~~hav~~ have got a race to day and I hope i come in a good plac.

Writing samples

Overall meaning
Ethan's writing has a clear message and ideas are linked. (1a = 8)

Use of genre
The recount genre has a clear beginning, middle and end and the genre is sustained throughout the piece. (1a = 6)

Grammar
Ethan writes in simple rather repetitive sentences and occasionally words are missing. (1b = 4)

Punctuation
Some sentences have a capital letter and a full stop. (1b = 2)

Vocabulary
Ethan adds some detail 'I came 42' though descriptions echo spoken language 'thay wur yummy'. (1b = 4)

Spelling
Ethan can spell some high-frequency words and cvc words 'when', 'come', but struggles with others 'thay', 'wur' and with more complex vocabulary 'cutrey', 'swets'. (1b = 4)

Handwriting
Other samples of Ethan's writing show that he forms his letters correctly and his writing is neat and uniform in size. (1a = 7)

Length of writing
Ethan has written approximately 80 words. (1a = 4)

Total score: 39
Overall, Ethan is working within 1a and should work on Writing Log 3.

Aisha, Writing Log 4, NC level 1a

The Mystryas box

a little girl called Sue
had a mystryas box. Sue was
5. She lived in London with her
Mum and dad. One day Sue
was watching the box when
Sudenly the box Started Moveing.
Sue was very exited so she
Looked inside. inside the box
ther was a teddy Sue was
very Happy She sowed her
Mum and dad thay wher
amast but the box nether
moved again.

Overall meaning
Ideas are linked in Aisha's story and the sequence is logical. (2c = 9)

Use of genre
The story has several actions and a clear ending. (2c = 7)

Grammar
Aisha uses mostly simple sentences with some compound sentences. (1a = 7)

Punctuation
Most sentences have a capital letter and a full stop. (1a = 3)

Vocabulary
Aisha's story shows some evidence of word selection, e.g. 'suddenly' 'amazed'. (1a = 6)

Spelling
She spells simple monosyllabic words correctly, e.g. 'was' 'will'. (1b = 5)

Handwriting
She forms all letters correctly and they are generally even in size. (1a = 8)

Length of writing
Aisha has written approximately 40 words. (1c = 2)

Total score: 44
Overall, Aisha is working at 1a and should work on Writing Log 4.

Writing samples

Taylor, Writing Log 5, NC level 2c

The naughty puppy

Once in a Little house ther was a girl calld Mia and a boy called Mike. Mia and Mike wher cosons. Thay playd togethr whenethr it was posible. Its rayning sed Mia good sed Mike. When evar it is raning pudle comes. pudle is a very naughty puppy. Just then mike herd a crek in the toy box Mike opend the lid of the toy box Look Mia Mike shawtid Its pudle, pudle Mia shawtid running acrost the room. When evar pudle cames ther all wase a naughty pudle to jump in. pudle tuk Mia and Mike owt side. pudle went arawnt a pudle. I think this is the one Mike sploshd in it getting Mia all mudy. Mia bendid dawn. Now pudle that was very naughty. Thay jumpd in to a very BIG pudle 123 jump Mia sed. Thay landid with a huge bump mike landid on his legs Mia landid on her side I need to werk on that she sed. Wher ar we sed Mia pudle barkd saying wher in the land of wite chocolat.

The End.

Overall meaning
Ideas are linked and the sequence is mostly logical. (2c = 9)

Use of genre
Taylor's story has characters and several actions but the ending strays into another genre and the story feels unfinished. (1a = 6)

Grammar
Taylor uses a variety of sentence openings and has some compound and complex sentence structures. (2c = 9)

Punctuation
About 50% of the sentences have a capital letter and full stop. She uses speech but no speech punctuation. (1a = 3)

Vocabulary
Some formulaic story language: 'Once in a little house …'; and the characters use appropriate speech: 'Now, Puddle,'; and some descriptive language: 'a creak in the toy box'. (1a = 6)

Spelling
She is able to spell some high-frequency words correctly 'just', 'little' though she has trouble with others 'thay' 'owt' and she struggles with more complex words 'shawtid' and with '-ed' endings. (1b = 5)

Handwriting
Her letters are generally correctly formed and orientated, although not of uniform size, and her use of capital letters is not consistent. (1b = 6)

Length of writing
Taylor has written approximately 175 words. (2a = 7)

Total score: 51
Overall Taylor is working at 2c, and she would benefit from a chance to secure her spelling and handwriting skills and so should work on Writing Log 5.

Writing samples

Fiona, Writing Log 6, NC level 2b

My best day
My best day was when I went to lego land. First we saw a sighn that said "wellcome" in lego. Then we paid to go in and went on a boat ride. Then me and my mum went on fairy tale brook. Then me, mum and my brother Alasdair went on pirate falls and me. Mum and Alasdair were soked. Then I went on the big dragon ride and I shouted "weeeeeeeeee". Then I went on a pirate climbing frame. Then I had a yummy lunch. Then I watch a pirate show. Then I went on a dinosore safarai park. Then I went on one of my favrate ride the vikings river splash! Then I went on the dino dipper.

Overall meaning
The sequence of this recount is logical. (2c = 9)

Use of genre
The recount answers who, what and where and the genre is sustained. (1a = 6)

Grammar
Fiona uses compound sentences which show consistency in tense but are simplistic and repetitive in style: 'Then me and mum…'. Some dialogue is introduced. (2c = 9)

Punctuation
Most simple and compound sentences are correctly punctuated. (3c = 9)

Vocabulary
Fiona uses some words for effect but these are generally limited to formulaic descriptions. (1a = 5)

Spelling
Fiona can spell high-frequency and simple regular words accurately and makes good attempts at less phonically regular words such as 'dinosore' and 'safarai'. (2b = 10)

Handwriting
Other samples of Fiona's writing show that she forms her letters correctly and her writing is neat and uniform in size. (2a = 11)

Length of writing
Fiona has written more than 100 words. (2c = 5)

Total score: 64
Overall, Fiona is working at the lower end of 2b and should start on Writing Log 6.

Chloe, Writing Log 7, NC level 2b

The naughty puppy
One day there was a puppy, this puppy was called Hannah. Hannah was very very naughty. She was rood. She barkt she rawld. The only thing to get her to be good was give her treets. The other bad thing was she wood never ever ever sleep. They slept out side. it so was not comftbual. The very next day they took hannah to the vet the vet said we might need to keep her hear only for one night. This time hannah was a bit scheard she whasant naughty.

Overall meaning
The ideas in Chloe's story are sequenced and developed and the writing relates to the title. (2a = 13)

Use of genre
Her story has a beginning and a middle but the end is a bit weak. (2c = 7)

Grammar
She writes mostly in simple sentences with some varied openings. (2b = 11)

Punctuation
Most sentences are correctly punctuated. (2a = 8)

Vocabulary
Chloe chooses some words and phrases for effect though these echo spoken language. (2b = 8)

Spelling
Chloe can spell many high-frequency words, though she needs support with some long vowel phonemes: e.g.'rood' and 'ed' endings: 'barkt'. (2b = 10)

Handwriting
Other samples of Chloe's writing show that she forms her letters correctly and her writing is neat and uniform in size. (3c = 12)

Length of writing
Chloe has written approximately 100 words. (2c = 5)

Total score: 74
Overall, Chloe is working within 2b and would benefit from starting on Writing Log 7.

Writing samples

Yasmin, Writing Log 8, NC level 2a

The naughty puppy
One day my mum asked me if I was aloud a pet what would it be? Amedietley I shouted "A DOG!" My mum looked at me and said come on then what are you waiting for lets go and get one. When we got to the pet shop I burst in looking for the dog section. Finnaly I got to the dog section looking for the perfect dog I looked thrue every ile until he came to the last pet it was a white and brown dog.

Overall meaning
Ideas are grouped in Yasmin's recount and the piece generally holds the reader's attention although it isn't strictly related to the title. (2b = 12)

Use of genre
Mostly accurate genre features e.g. chronological order; time connectives; past tense. (2a = 9)

Grammar
Yasmin uses some variation in sentence openings for effect: 'Amedietley I shouted'. (2b = 11)

Punctuation
Her punctuation is generally secure, with use of question marks and exclamation marks and occasional use of speech marks. (2b = 7)

Vocabulary
Yasmin's writing shows more adventurous word choices and strong verbs: 'I burst in'. (3c = 12)

Spelling
Yasmin can spell most high-frequency words and some more complex words 'section' and makes a good phonic representation of less common words 'aloud', 'aisle'. (3c = 14)

Handwriting
Other samples of Yasmin's writing show that she forms her letters correctly and her writing is legible, neat and looks fluent. (3c = 12)

Length of writing
Yasmin's has written approximately 90 words. (1a = 4)

Total score: 81
Overall, Yasmin shows features of writing at 2a and she should start on Writing Log 8.

Pupil name ________________ Term _____ TA name ________________

Pupil Progress Tracker

Date	Rapid Stage and Writing Log	Session title	Software session completed?	Notes about writing	Notes for next session

Group name ______________ Term ___ TA name ______________

Group Progress Tracker

Child's name	NC level at start	Target NC level	Final NC level	Sub-level difference	Rapid Writing Stage and Log at start	Rapid Writing Stage and Log at end	Stage and Set difference	Number of guided reading sessions	Number of computer sessions

Yearly Progress Tracker

Name:____________________	Rapid Stage and Writing Log	NC sub-level
Term 1		
Term 2		
Term 3		
Term 4		
Term 5		
Term 6		
Name:____________________	Rapid Stage and Writing Log	NC sub-level
Term 1		
Term 2		
Term 3		
Term 4		
Term 5		
Term 6		
Name:____________________	Rapid Stage and Writing Log	NC sub-level
Term 1		
Term 2		
Term 3		
Term 4		
Term 5		
Term 6		
Name:____________________	Rapid Stage and Writing Log	NC sub-level
Term 1		
Term 2		
Term 3		
Term 4		
Term 5		
Term 6		

Note: This chart is based on a six-term year (six half terms).

Rapid Maths

Rapid Maths provides enjoyable and well-structured materials divided into five levels for pupils aged 6 to 11 who have difficulty with mathematics, and in particular with number.

Rapid Maths is structured around **five colour levels**. Each of these is divided further into **three parts** which mark the progressive steps that children need to take in order to grasp number concepts. In order to ensure excellent progress, children should use the pupil books and copymasters and then practise their skills using the games software and homework activities.

Rapid Maths Colour Stage	England and Wales NC level	Scottish CfE Level	Northern Ireland Curriculum Level
Red Level Stage 1	Completing Level 1 and beginning to work on Level 2	First Level	Level 1
Blue Level Stage 2	Working on Level 2	First Level	Level 2
Green Level Stage 3	Consolidating Level 2 and beginning to work on Level 3	First Level	Level 2, Working towards Level 3
Yellow Level Stage 4	Some revising of Level 2 but mostly working on Level 3	First/Second Level	Level 3
Purple Level Stage 5	Comfortable with most of Level 3, working towards Level 4	First/Second Level	Level 3

Checking counting

The ability to count groups of objects accurately is central to children's understanding of the number system, so checking the child's ability to count is a good way of determining their best starting point. A very useful 'rule of thumb' for children who are having difficulty is to keep the numbers they work with in arithmetic smaller than the biggest number of objects they can count accurately and consistently. As the child's counting improves, you can increase the size of numbers they use for addition, subtraction, multiplication and division.

Each part of a Rapid Maths pupil book is structured to take account of this 'rule of thumb'. For example, Red Level Pupil Book Part 2 includes: Counting to 20; Addition and subtraction within 12; Mental recall of number bonds to 6.

Children need to be able to count:

- in ones, twos and tens forwards and backwards
- in tens and ones (for example, if they are given 43 items, as well as being able to count them individually: '1, 2, 3, 4, ...39, 40, 41, 42, 43', they eventually need to be able to group them in tens and some ones, and count '10, 20, 30, 40, 41, 42, 43'.

Check the child's counting using real items to count – don't just ask the child to recite the number names. You will be most successful if you start with small numbers and build up to larger ones, rather than risking starting too high, and having the child fail at the start.

Counting money is something most children are keen to do. Real money is much better than plastic or card coins, and children will not feel it is 'babyish'. Also, a £1 bag of real pennies (from the post office or a bank) is usually cheaper than a bag of 100 plastic pennies!

Starting with the child

When you have a new child starting on the Rapid Maths programme, whether they are new to the programme or new to your class, follow the steps below to ensure that they are on the right path to achieving and feeling more confident in maths.

1 *Which colour level is best?*

a **If you know the child:** Use the Teacher Assessment Chart on page 33 to establish which Rapid Maths colour level the child should start at. If you are unsure, use the Counting Assessment Tasks on page 34. NB: A child who is not yet working at NC Level 1 will need further practical experience with counting before starting on these materials. Go to section 2 (page 34).

Ensuring confidence

Remember that it is best to start a child on a part of the programme where they are confident, even if it means they will start by completing work they find fairly straightforward. This can help you set an expectation of a good pace of work, and will build the child's confidence and motivation.

Placing children in the Rapid Maths programme

Teacher assessment chart

If the child is comfortable with:	Prior Teacher Assessment of child's NC Level (England) before starting	Rapid Maths Colour Stage
▸ counting to 10 ▸ reading numbers up to 10 ▸ arithmetic involving one more or one less	Completing Level 1 and beginning to work on Level 2 →	Red Level/ Stage 1
▸ counting and place value with numbers to 35 ▸ arithmetic within 15 ▸ mental recall of number bonds to 7	Working on Level 2 →	Blue Level/ Stage 2
▸ counting and place value with numbers to 75 ▸ arithmetic within 40 ▸ mental recall of number bonds to 10	Consolidating Level 2, and beginning to work on Level 3 →	Green Level/ Stage 3
▸ counting and place value with numbers to 120 ▸ arithmetic within 60 ▸ mental recall of number bonds to 15	Some revising of Level 2, but mostly working on Level 3 →	Yellow Level/ Stage 4
▸ counting and place value with numbers to 200 ▸ arithmetic within 120 ▸ mental recall of number bonds to 20 ▸ mental recall of tables facts to 6 x 6, and all 2s, 5s and 10s	Comfortable with most of Level 3; Working towards Level 4 →	Purple Level/ Stage 5

b **If the child is new to you:** Use the Counting Assessment Tasks on page 34 as a guide to help you start to identify the correct colour level of Rapid Maths for the child.

Counting assessment tasks

These counting assessment tasks are very straightforward, and are organised in five stages to match the five colour levels of Rapid Maths. Start at the beginning, and continue for as many tasks as the child can complete confidently, accurately and reasonably quickly.

For the complete set of tasks, you need:

100 × real 1p coins	5 × plastic or card £1 coins
6 × real 10p coins	18 × token £10 notes
20 × real 2p coins	(Make £10 notes using page P29 in the Purple Copymasters)

You may wish to put a clean sheet of paper (A3 size) on the table in front of the child to give them a clearly defined working space for their counting. For each question, put a pile of coins or notes appropriate to the question on the paper for the child to help themselves. Stop as soon as you feel you have reached the highest level task that the child can achieve.

Counting assessment tasks			
Task	**Money needed**	**Ask the child...**	**Rapid Maths level/ stage**
1	About 20 x 1p coins	Can you give me 9 pence?	Red Level/ Stage 1
2	11 × 1p coins	How much is there here?	Red Level/ Stage 1
3	28 ×1p coins	How much is there here?	Red Level/ Stage 1
4	About 50 × 1p coins	Can you give me 34p?	Blue Level/ Stage 2
5	4 × 10p coins and 2 × 1p coins: total 42p	How much is there here?	Blue Level/ Stage 2
6	4 × 10p coins and 16 × 1p coins: total 56p	How much is there here?	Blue Level/ Stage 2
7	95 × 1p coins	How much is there here?	Green Level/ Stage 3
8	6 × 10p coins and 20 × 1p coins	Can you give me 70p?	Green Level/ Stage 3
9	20 × 2p coins	Can you give me 34p?	Green Level/ Stage 3
10	9 × £10 notes	How much is there here?	Yellow Level/ Stage 4
11	18 × £10 notes	Can you give me £140?	Yellow Level/ Stage 4
12	16 × £10 notes and 4 × £1 coins: total £164	How much is there here?	Yellow Level/ Stage 4
13	18 × £10 notes and 5 × £1 coins	Can you give me £183?	Purple Level/ Stage 5
14	18 × £10 notes, 3 × £1, 3 × 10p coins and 14 × 1p: total £183.44	How much is there here?	Purple Level/ Stage 5

2 Can the child move straight on to Part 2 or Part 3 of their colour level?

Start with the Progress Test for Part 1 of the colour level that is indicated by the child's work in the Counting Assessment Tasks, or by your teacher assessment. The **Progress tests** are provided in the Rapid Teaching Guide for each level, and one version of each is also reproduced in this book, for your convenience:

a **Red Level** (see pages 36–38)
b **Blue Level** (see pages 39–41)
c **Green Level** (see pages 42–44)
d **Yellow Level** (see pages 45–47)
e **Purple Level** (see pages 48–50)

Each colour level has three tests, matching the three parts of the pupil materials. There is more detailed information about the Progress Tests on page 17 of the Teaching Guide for each colour level.

Checking understanding

It is also important to be aware that many children who have difficulties will have gaps in their understanding and skills that need addressing, if they are going to make sustained progress. The Progress tests will help you check on key topics in an organised manner.

If needed, read the questions on the test to the child, and provide rough paper.

- If the child scores 9 or 10 on the test you have given them, try the next level test, too.
- If the child scores less than 5, backtrack and try the test at a previous (lower) level (or stop, if the child has already completed that one).

Your aim is to find the 'best fit' of colour level and part of the book for the child to start on, and you need to ensure the child is fully confident and secure in their answers for that level.

For more suggestions on how to assess a child's knowledge before starting them on the programme see the 'Getting Started' section of the Teaching Guide for each colour level.

Examples

Example 1:
Harry has completed the counting tasks successfully up to Task 8, which suggests he should start at Green Level. His teacher gives him the Green Progress Test for Part 1, and he gets 9 questions right; he tries Green Test Part 2, and gets 9 right again; when he tries the Part 3 test, he scores 5. The best place for Harry to start is at the beginning of Part 2 of the Green materials.

Example 2:
Lauren reached counting task 5, which suggests she should start at Blue Level. However, when she does the Blue Progress Test for Part 1, she only gets 3 questions correct. Her teacher decides to give her the Red Level Test for Part 1, and she scores 8, so the teacher decides it is best to start her at the beginning of Red Level, as there seem to be considerable gaps in her understanding of addition and subtraction. Lauren is likely to work quite quickly through the first part of the Red materials, and may be able to miss out some sections. Her teacher can keep track of this very easily on the Record Sheets provided at the back of the Teaching Guide.

Checking handwriting of numerals

Some children are held back because their number formation is so poor that even they cannot read it accurately! Some may still be having difficulty with reversals, or with particular numbers – for example, many children find it difficult to write a 5 clearly. Good handwriting habits will help a child work more confidently and speedily. Whatever colour level a child is working on, some attention to poor handwriting can be very helpful.

There is guidance on checking and improving handwriting in the Red Level Teaching Guide, on page 9, and there are several copymasters in Red Level that provide useful practice in a variety of ways. For example, Red Level Copymasters R34 and R35 show a standard method of writing each numeral, and give a structure for a week's practice.

3 Ongoing assessment

You can keep track of the child's progress using the progress trackers on pages 51–55 of this book. You can also use the Record Sheets at the end of each Teaching Guide which allow the children to self-evaluate and the adult working with the child to log which activities and pages they have completed.

Once a child has finished a part of a book, give them the corresponding Progress Test to check their progress. There is a photocopiable Certificate of Achievement on page 56 of this book, which can be given to the child to take home to show parents or carers.

Name: ______________________ Date: ______________________

Progress test Red Pupil Book Part 1 Version A

1 How many buttons? _____

2 Which number is under my finger? _____

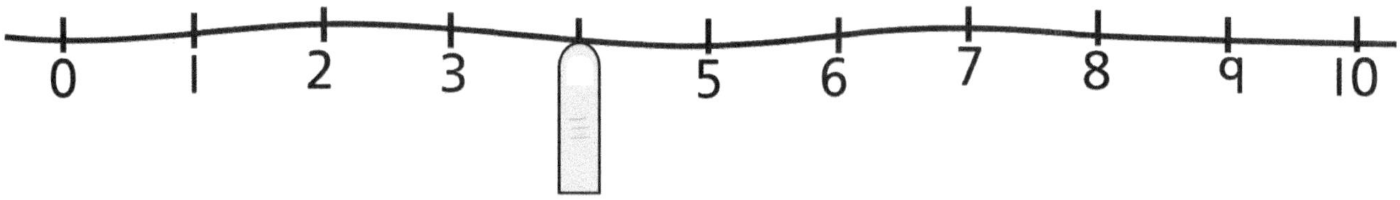

3 Which number is under my finger? _____

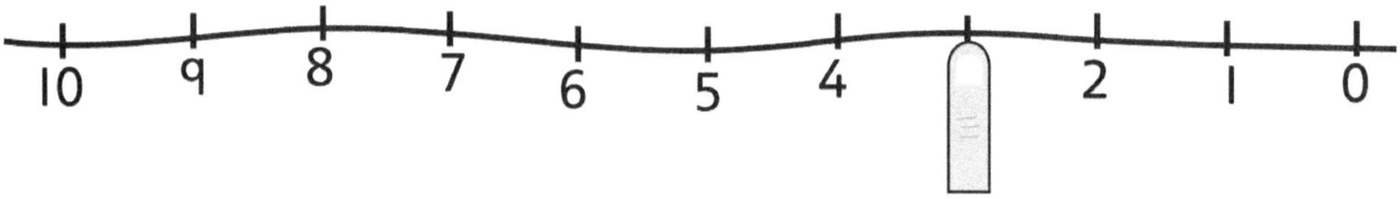

Write the missing numbers.

4

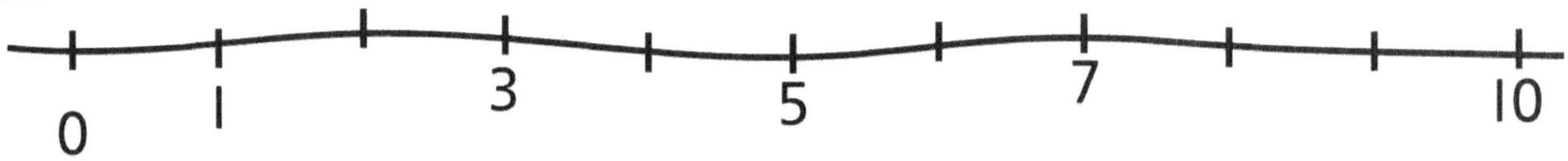

5

6 4 + 1 = _____

7 2 + 2 = _____

9 5 – 2 = _____

10 3 + 4 = _____

Name: ____________________ Date: ____________________

Progress test Red Pupil Book Part 2 Version A

1 How many counters? _____

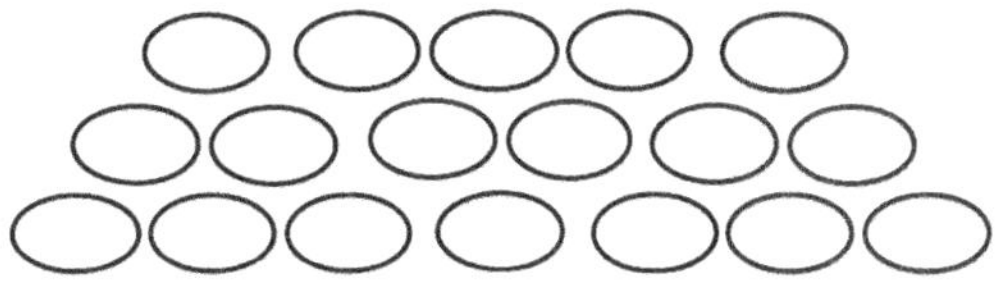

2 How many pencils? _____

3 Write the missing numbers.

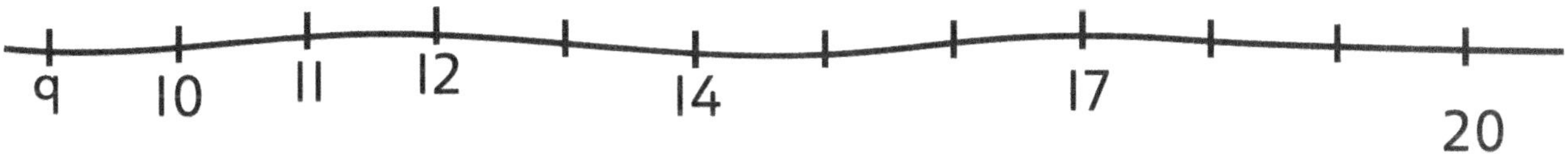

4 7 + 4 = _____

5 9 – 3 = _____

6 8 – 5 = _____

7 6 + 6 = _____

Share these fish between 2.

8 How many fish each? _____

9 Is there one left over? _____

10 How many carrots altogether? _____

Progress test Red Pupil Book Part 3 Version A

1 How many marbles? _____

2 How much money? _____

3 Write the missing numbers.

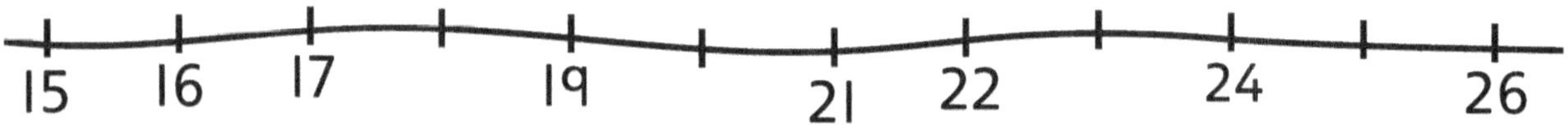

4 7 + 6 = _____

5 12 – 4 = _____

6 15 – 6 = _____

7 8 + ☐ = 11

What comes next?

8 2, 4, 6, 8, 10, 12, 14, _____

9 5, 10, 15, _____

3 bean bags

10 What is his score? _____

Name: ____________________ Date: ____________________

Progress test Blue Pupil Book Part 1 Version A

1 How many candles? _____

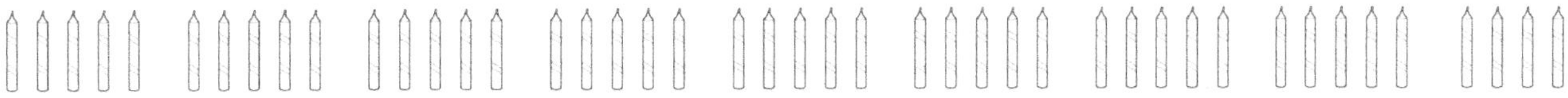

2 Write these numbers as words:

10 8 7

_______________ _______________ _______________

Write the missing numbers:

3 34, 33, 32, 31, _____ , _____ , _____ , _____

4 2 + ☐ = 8

5 7 + 9 = _____

6 22, 24, 26, 28, _____ , _____ , _____ , _____

One spider needs 10 pipecleaners.

7 How many pipecleaners for 5 spiders? _____

8

____

9 How much money? _______

10 4 × 5 = _______

Name: ____________________ Date: ____________________

Progress test Blue Pupil Book Part 2 Version A

1 How much money? _____

2 Write these numbers as words:

11 15 18

____________ ____________ ____________

3 This is 24.

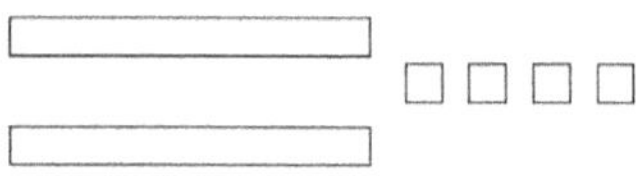

Draw 47:

Write the missing numbers:

4 $6 \times 2 = \square$

5 $\square \times 2 = 20$

6 $6 \times 5 = \square$

7 $12 + 7 = \square$

8 $19 - 8 = \square$

9

What is the time?

____

10 Score 3 points for each frog.

How many points for 5 frogs?

____

Name: ____________________ Date: ____________________

Progress test Blue Pupil Book Part 3 Version A

1 How many ants? _____

2 Write these numbers as words:

30 40 70

________________ ________________ ________________

Write the missing numbers:

3 15, 20, 25, 30, _____ , _____ , _____ , _____

4 3 + ☐ = 10

5 6 × 3 = _____

6

How many toys for £8?

____

7 10 ÷ 2 = _____

8 How much money? _____

Draw tens and ones to help you.

9 14 + 13 = _____

10 27 – 12 = _____

Name: ____________________ Date: ____________________

Progress test Green Pupil Book Part 1 Version A

1 This is 24.

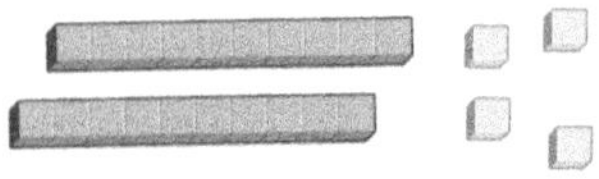

How many is this? _____

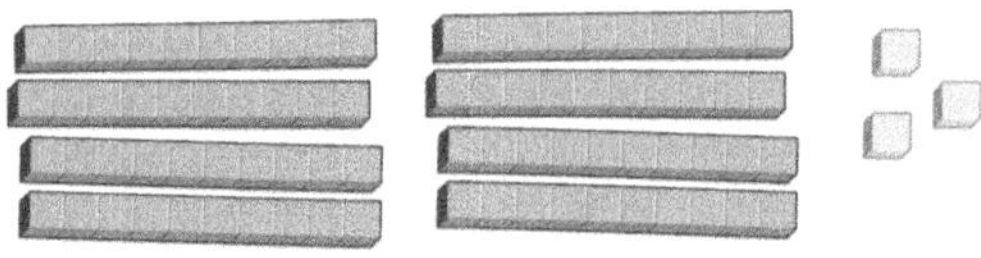

2 Write these numbers as words:

84 ____________________________

72 ____________________________

Write the missing numbers:

3

90, 80, 70, ____ , ____ , ____

5 $3 \times 5 =$ _____

$4 \times 2 =$ _____

4 $5 + \square = 11$

$\square + 3 = 12$

6 $16 \div 2 =$ _____

$25 \div 5 =$ _____

7

How much change? ______________

Draw tens and ones to help you.

8 What is half of 46? ______

9 27 + 15

10 42 − 23

Name: ____________________ Date: ____________________

Progress test Green Pupil Book Part 2 Version A

1 This is 32.

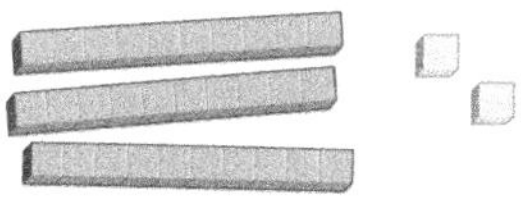

How many is this? ________

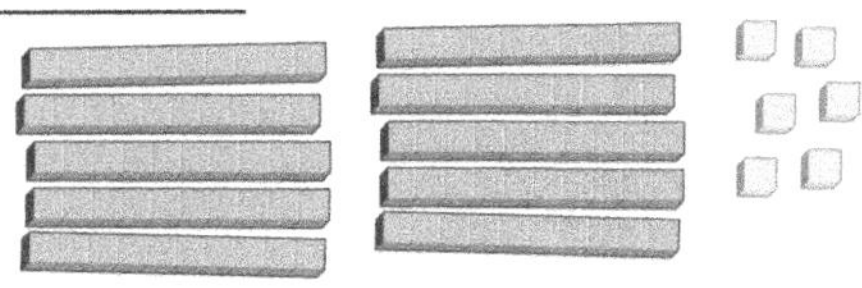

2 How much money? ____________

3

____

Write the missing numbers:

4 6 + ☐ = 13 ☐ + 5 = 14

5 7 × 5 = _____

4 × 6 = _____

6 12 ÷ 3 = _____

14 ÷ 2 = _____

7

____

Draw tens and ones to help you.

8 What is double 19? ______

9 53 – 38

10 27 + 26

Name: ____________________ Date: ____________________

Progress test Green Pupil Book Part 3 Version A

1 This is 14.

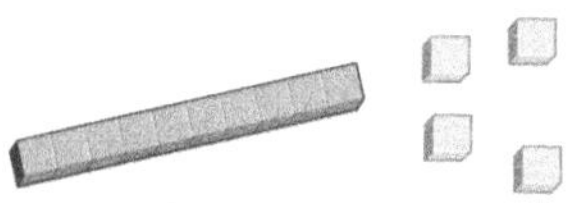

How many is this? ____________

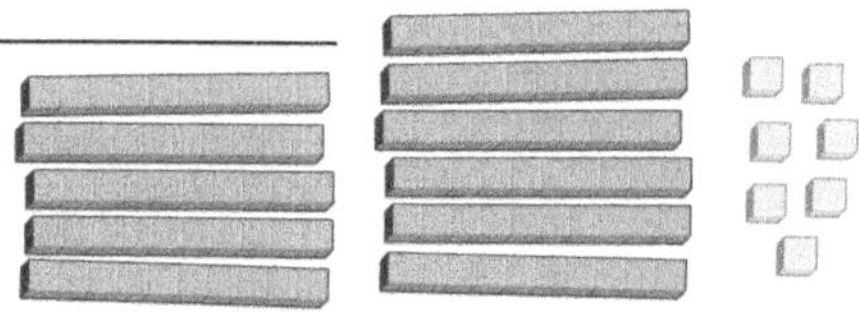

2 How many is a century? ____________

How many is a dozen? ____________

Write the missing numbers:

3 $5 \times 7 =$ _____

$4 \times 8 =$ _____

4 $20 \div 2 =$ _____

$24 \div 3 =$ _____

5 58, 68, 78, 88, ______, ______, ______

97, 87, 77, 67, ______, ______, ______

6

____

7

____

8

How many minutes till 6 o'clock? ____________

9 $37 + 14$

10 $56 - 28$

Name: ______________________ Date: ______________________

Progress test Yellow Pupil Book Part 1 Version A

1 This is 23.

How many is this? _____

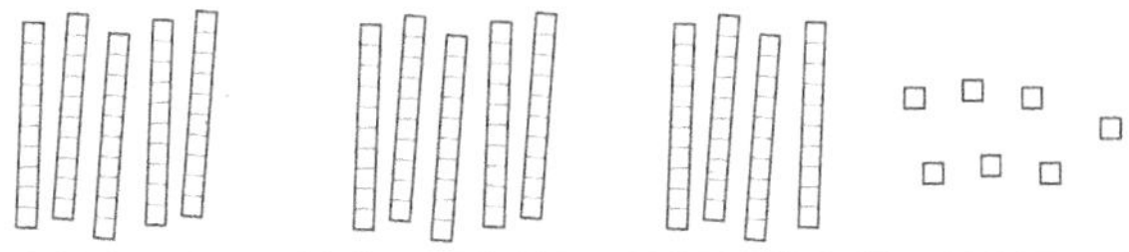

2 Write each date the other way.

3rd September 2010 is ______________

18/5/09 is ____________________________

Write the missing numbers.

3 $2 \times 9 =$ ______

$6 \times 0 =$ ______

$6 \times 6 =$ ______

4 $20 \div 5 =$ ______

$27 \div 3 =$ ______

$16 \div 4 =$ ______

5

____

6

____

7 5 pies in a pack. How many pies in 6 packs? ______

8 What is $\frac{1}{2}$ of 64p? ______ What is $\frac{1}{4}$ of 64p? ______

9

$$\begin{array}{r} 26 \\ \times\ 3 \\ \hline \end{array}$$

10

$$\begin{array}{r} 27 \\ \times\ 2 \\ \hline \end{array}$$

Progress test Yellow Pupil Book Part 2 Version A

1 This is 134. How much is this? __________

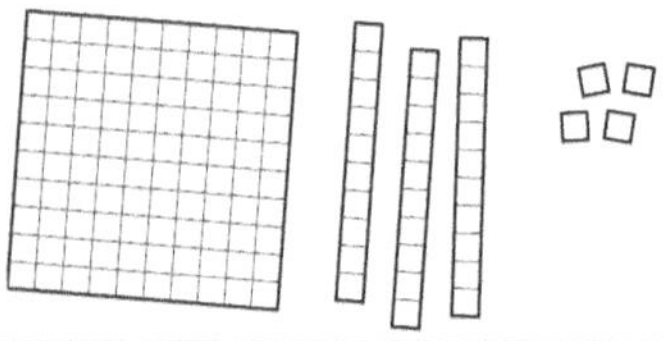

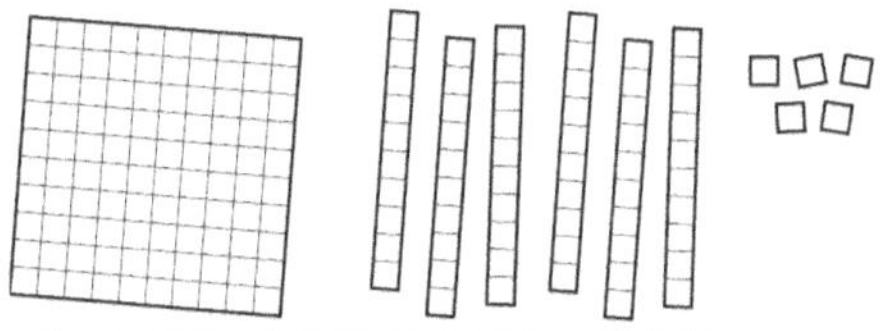

2 How much did these cost in the sale?

Write the missing numbers.

3 $10 \times 6 =$ ______

$5 \times 8 =$ ______

4 $18 \div 3 =$ ______

$28 \div 4 =$ ______

5 $29 + 40 =$ ☐

$47 +$ ☐ $= 100$

6 $2\overline{)59}$

7

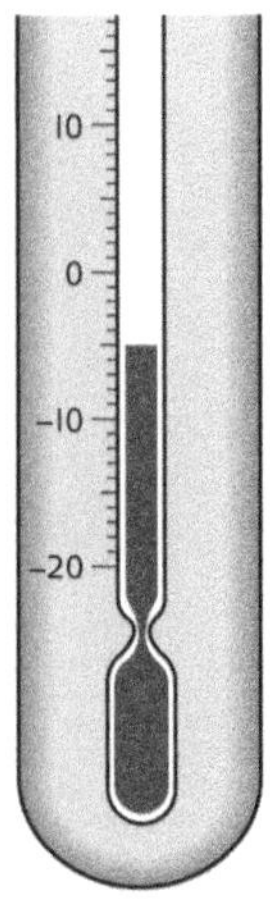

____

8

```
  27
×  3
────
```

9

```
  32
  28
+ 36
────

────
```

10 100 – 34

Name: ____________________ Date: ____________________

Progress test Yellow Pupil Book Part 3 Version A

1 This is 142. How much is this? ____________

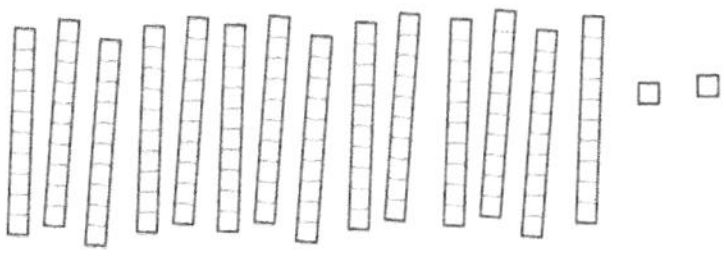

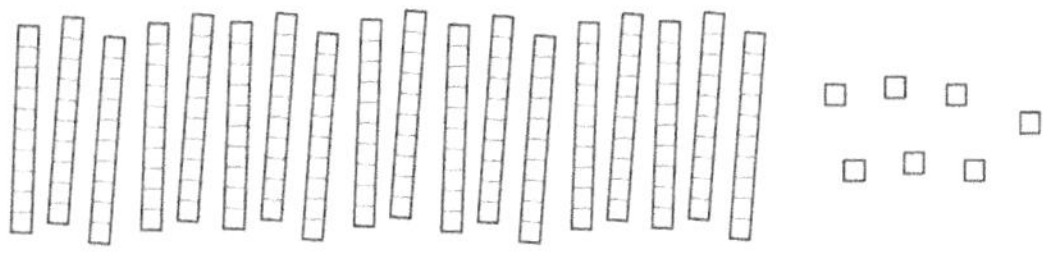

2

I've saved £19.
How much more do I need?

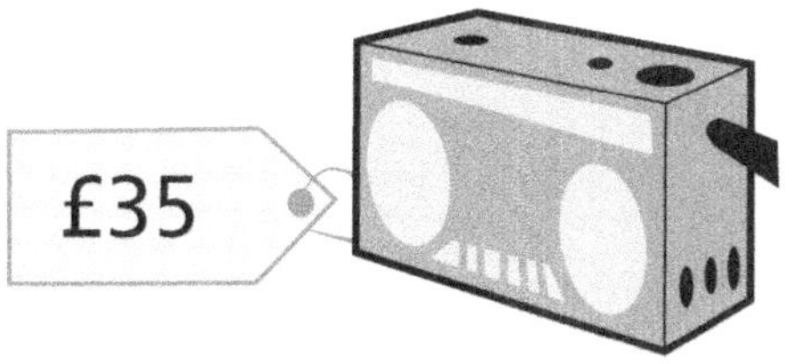

____

3

I've saved £4 a month, for 7 months.
How much have I saved altogether?

____

4 Write the missing numbers.

$\frac{1}{2}$, 1, $1\frac{1}{2}$, 2, ______, 3, ______, 4

5 Is each piece $\frac{1}{4}$? Write <u>Yes</u> or <u>No</u>.

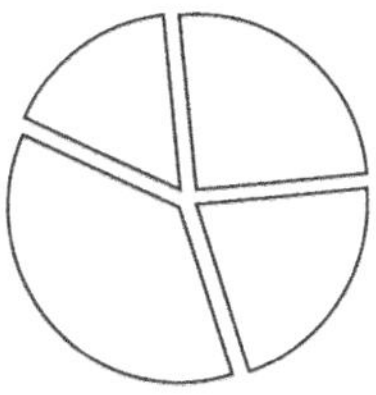

____

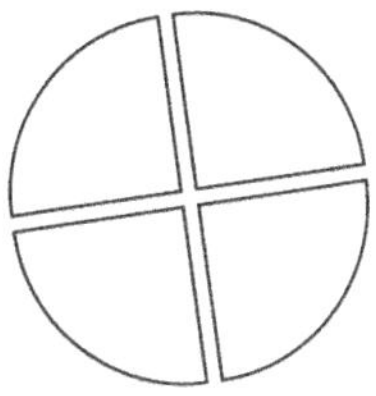

____

6 $3 \times 9 =$ ______

$30 \div 6 =$ ______

7 $3\overline{)74}$

8

$$\begin{array}{r} 28 \\ \times \quad 4 \\ \hline \end{array}$$

9

$$\begin{array}{r} 19 \\ +\ 84 \\ \hline \\ \hline \end{array}$$

10 100 – 57

Name: ____________________ Date: ____________________

Progress test Purple Pupil Book Part 1 Version A

1 This is £23.

How much is this? ________

2 Write the missing numbers.

152, 162, 172, 182, _____ , _____ , _____ , 222.

3

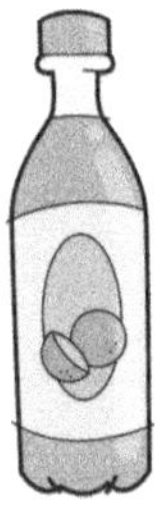

Each bottle of squash will make 40 cups.
How many cups will 5 bottles make? ________

4 $8 \times 6 =$ ________ $36 \div 6 =$ ________

5

Fill in the missing fractions.

________ eaten.

________ left.

6

$$\begin{array}{r} 59 \\ \times\ \ 4 \\ \hline \end{array}$$

7

$$2\,\overline{)\,293}$$

8 $255 \div 3$

9 How much altogether? ________

10 How much change from £10? ________

Name: ______________________ Date: ____________________

Progress test Purple Pupil Book Part 2 Version A

1 This is 124.

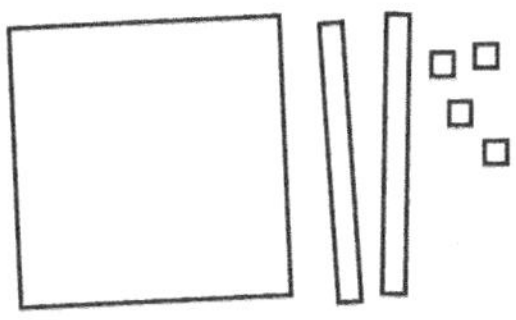

How much is this? ________

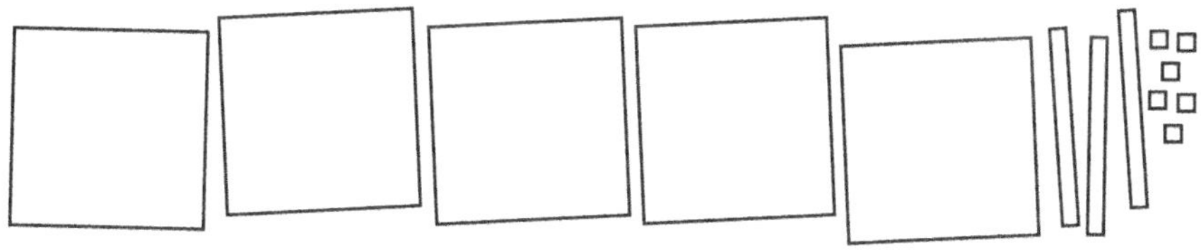

2 25 chalks in a box.
How many chalks in 6 boxes? ________

3 **248**

Write this number in words.

____

4

```
  292
- 178
 ____

 ____
```

5 Add these:

278 **62**

____

6 What is the difference between …

70 and 40? ________

245 and 102? ________

7 How long is this mouse's tail?
Write the length in 2 different ways.

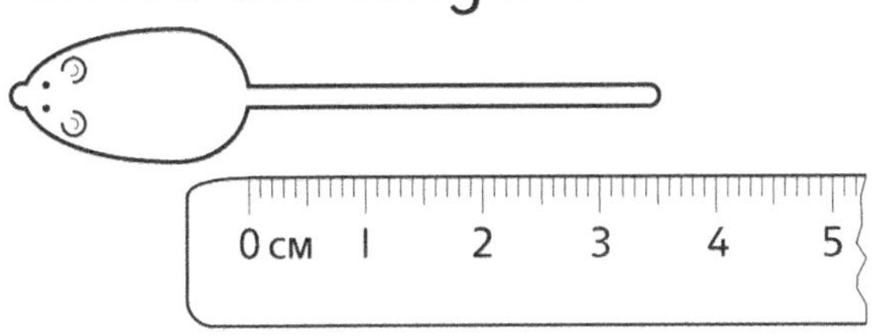

________ cm ________ cm

8

```
  76
×  4
 ___
```

```
 102
×  3
 ___
```

9

2) 473

10 What is double 177? ____________

Name: ______________ Date: ______________

Progress test Purple Pupil Book Part 3 Version A

1 This is 114.

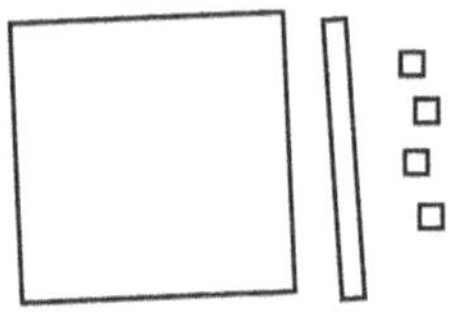

How much is this? __________

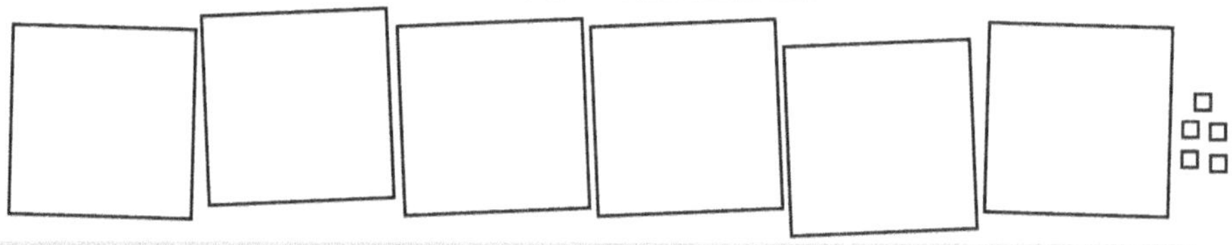

2 Which number is the arrow pointing to? __________

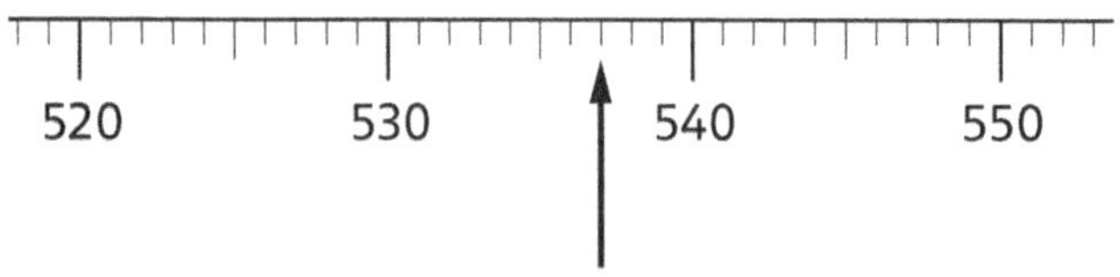

3 Round each number to the nearest ten.

427 __________ 799 __________ 253 __________

4

20 paperclips in each box.
I want 140 paperclips.
How many boxes do I need?

____

5 6 9 3 + 1 5 8

6 4 5 0 − 1 8 2

7

I've got £3·50, minus £1·40 bus fare.
How much have I got?

____

8

$$\begin{array}{r} 178 \\ \times \quad 4 \\ \hline \end{array} \qquad \begin{array}{r} 92 \\ \times \ 6 \\ \hline \end{array}$$

9 £745 ÷ 3

10 What is 50% of …

£27? __________ £18·50? __________

Name ______________________________

Progress Tracker: Red

	Date of assessment			
The chart helps you to summarise the progress the child is making whilst using the Red Level of Rapid Maths.	**Working towards**	**Reasonably confident**	**Totally confident**	**Progress tests**
Red Part 1				
Counting to 12 (in 1s, forwards and backwards)				See page 36
Writing numerals 0 to 9				
Addition and subtraction within 7				
Mental recall of number bonds to 5				
Using a number line, forwards and backwards				
Red Part 2				
Counting to 20 (in 1s and 2s)				See page 37
Addition and subtraction within 12				
Mental recall of number bonds to 6				
Sharing between 2 within 12				
Multiples of 3 to 12				
Red Part 3				
Counting to 35 (in 1s and 2s)				
Writing numbers 10 to 20				See page 38
Using money (1p, 2p, £1 and £10) and writing £ sign				
Addition and subtraction within 15				
Mental recall of number bonds to 7				
Odd and even numbers to 35				
Multiples of 2, 5 and 10, to 35				

By the end of Red Level children will:
have achieved NC Level 1 and be working within NC Level 2. CfE: First Level

Name ______________________

Progress Tracker: Blue

	Date of assessment			
The chart helps you to summarise the progress the child is making whilst using the Blue Level of Rapid Maths.	**Working towards**	**Reasonably confident**	**Totally confident**	**Progress tests**
Blue Part 1				
Counting to 50				See page 39
Grouping in tens				
Spelling numbers one to ten				
Ordinal numbers: 1st, 2nd, 3rd, 4th				
Using money (1p, 2p, 5p, £1 and £10)				
Addition and subtraction within 20				
Mental recall of number bonds to 8				
Multiples of 2, 5 and 10 to 50				
Blue Part 2				
Counting to 60				See page 40
Grouping in tens				
Reading and spelling numbers eleven to twenty				
Using money (1p, 5p, 10p, £1, £5, £10)				
Addition and subtraction within 24 (in 1s) and 50 (in 5s and 10s)				
Mental recall of number bonds to 9				
Multiples of 3 to 18, and of 2, 5 and 10 to 50				
Using $\frac{1}{2}$ (half-hours on clock)				
Ordinal numbers: 1st to 12th				
Blue Part 3				
Counting to 75				
Reading and spelling thirty to seventy-five				See page 41
Using money (1p, 2p, 5p, 10p, 50p, £1)				
Addition and subtraction within 40				
Mental recall of number bonds to 10				
Multiples of 3 to 30; 2 and 5 to 50; 10 to 70				
Division (including symbol ÷)				
By the end of Blue Level children will: be confidently working within NC Level 2. CfE: First Level				

Name ______________________________

Progress Tracker: Green

	Date of assessment			
The chart helps you to summarise the progress the child is making whilst using the Green Level of Rapid Maths.	**Working towards**	**Reasonably confident**	**Totally confident**	**Progress tests**
Green Part 1				
Counting to 100				See page 42
Reading and spelling 70 to 100				
Using money (change from 50p)				
Addition and subtraction within 50				
Mental recall to 11 and to 12				
Multiples of 2 and 5 to 50, 10 to 100, 3 to 30, 4 to 20				
Halves of a group				
Green Part 2				
Counting to 110				See page 43
Reading and spelling 101 to 110				
Using money (amounts below and above £1)				
Addition and subtraction within 55				
Mental recall to 13 and to 14				
Multiples of 2 and 5 to 50, 10 to 100, 3 to 30, 4 to 24				
Halves of a group (with remainders, $\frac{1}{2}$ or 0.5)				
Green Part 3				
Counting to 120				
Reading and spelling to 120				See page 44
Using money (bills and change)				
Addition and subtraction within 60				
Mental recall to 15				
Multiples of 2 and 5 to 50, 10 to 100, 3 to 30, 4 to 40				
Division (including halving)				
Using $\frac{1}{4}$ (quarter-hours on a clock)				
By the end of Green Level children will: have achieved NC Level 2 and be working within NC Level 3 CfE: First Level				

Name ____

Progress Tracker: Yellow

	Date of assessment			
The chart helps you to summarise the progress the child is making whilst using the Yellow Level of Rapid Maths.	**Working towards**	**Reasonably confident**	**Totally confident**	**Progress tests**
Yellow Part 1				
Counting to 150				See page 45
Using money (giving change)				
Addition and subtraction within 80				
Mental recall of tables facts: all of the 0, 1, 2 and 10 times tables, and 3s, 4s and 5s within 25				
Ordinal numbers (1st to 31st)				
$\frac{1}{2}$s and $\frac{1}{4}$s				
Multiplying 2-digit numbers by 2 or 3 within 80				
Yellow Part 2				
Counting to 180				See page 46
Using money (half prices)				
Addition and subtraction within 100				
Mental recall of tables facts: all of the 0, 1, 2, 3, 4, 5 and 10 times tables				
Multiples of 6 to 60				
Multiplying by 2, 3, 4 and 5 within 100				
Dividing by 2 within 100				
Negative numbers				
Yellow Part 3				
Counting to 200				
Using money (bills and giving change)				See page 47
Addition and subtraction within 120				
Mental recall of tables facts: all of the 0, 1, 2, 3, 4, 5 and 10 times tables, and 6s within 36				
Mental recall of number bonds within 20				
Multiplying and dividing by 2, 3, 5 and 10 within 120				
$\frac{1}{2}$s, $\frac{1}{4}$s, $\frac{1}{3}$rds and $\frac{1}{5}$ths				
By the end of Yellow Level children will: be working confidently within NC Level 3. CfE: First/Second Level				

Name ______________________________

Progress Tracker: Purple

	Date of assessment			
The chart helps you to summarise the progress the child is making whilst using the Purple Level of Rapid Maths.	**Working towards**	**Reasonably confident**	**Totally confident**	**Progress tests**
Purple Part 1				
Counting to 500				
Using money (using notes and coins)				
Addition and subtraction within 300				
Mental recall of number bonds within 20 (consolidation)				
Mental recall of tables facts: all of the 0, 1, 2, 3, 4, 5, 6 and 10 times tables				See page 48
Multiples of 9 to 90				
Multiplication and division within 300, by 2, 3, 4, 5 and 10				
$\frac{1}{2}$s , $\frac{1}{4}$s, $\frac{1}{3}$rds and $\frac{1}{5}$ths				
Purple Part 2				
Counting to 800				
Using money (dividing amounts by 3)				
Addition and subtraction within 500				
Reading and spelling numbers to 500				See page 49
Mental recall of tables facts: all of the 0, 1, 2, 3, 4, 5, 6, 9 and 10 times tables				
Multiples of 7 to 70				
Multiplication and division within 500, especially by 2, 3, 4, 5 and 10				
Purple Part 3				
Counting to 1000				
Using money (rounding and rough answers)				
Addition and subtraction within 1000				
Reading and spelling numbers to 1000				See page 50
Mental recall of tables facts: all up to 10 × 10				
Multiples of 8 to 80				
Multiplication and division within 750, especially by 2, 3, 4, 5 and 10				
Fractions: $\frac{1}{2}$s, $\frac{1}{4}$s, $\frac{1}{10}$s				
By the end of Purple Level children will: have achieved NC Level 3 and be working within NC Level 4. CfE: First/Second Level				

Certificate of Achievement

Well done to

....

for your great Achievement